PARIS SAINT-GERMAIN

BY
MARK STEWART

NORWOODHOUSE PRESS

Chicago, Illinois

NORWOODHOUSE PRESS

P.O. Box 316598 • Chicago, Illinois 60631
For more information about Norwood House Press please visit our website at
www.norwoodhousepress.com or call 866-565-2900.

Photography and Collectibles:
The trading cards and other memorabilia assembled in the background for this book's cover and interior pages
are all part of the author's collection and are reproduced for educational and artistic purposes.

All photos courtesy of Associated Press except the following individual photos and artifacts (page numbers):
Figurine Panini (6, 10, 17), LFP/Panini (10 bottom), Topps, Inc. (11 top, 22), Panini America Inc. (11 middle),
Panini SpA (11 bottom).

Cover image: Christophe Saidi/SIPA via AP Images

Designer: Ron Jaffe
Series Editor: Mike Kennedy
Content Consultants: Michael Jacobsen and Jonathan Wentworth-Ping
Project Management: Black Book Partners, LLC
Editorial Production: Lisa Walsh

LIBRARY OF CONGRESS CATALOGING-IN-PUBLICATION DATA
Names: Stewart, Mark, 1960 July 7- author.
Title: Paris Saint-Germain / By Mark Stewart.
Description: Chicago, Illinois : Norwood House Press, 2017. | Series: First
   Touch Soccer | Includes bibliographical references and index. | Audience:
   Age 5-8. | Audience: K to Grade 3.
Identifiers: LCCN 2016058217 (print) | LCCN 2017005791 (ebook) | ISBN
   9781599538617 (library edition : alk. paper) | ISBN 9781684040803 (eBook)
Subjects: LCSH: Paris-Saint-Germain-Football-Club--History--Juvenile
   literature.
Classification: LCC GV943.6.P37 S84 2017 (print) | LCC GV943.6.P37 (ebook) |
   DDC 796.334/640944361--dc23
LC record available at https://lccn.loc.gov/2016058217

This publication is intended for educational purposes and is not affiliated with any team, league, or association
including: Paris Saint-Germain Football Club, Federation Francaise de Football, Ligue 1, The Union of European
Football Associations (UEFA), or the Federation Internationale de Football Association (FIFA).

302N--072017
Manufactured in the United States of America in North Mankato, Minnesota.

CONTENTS

Meet Paris Saint-Germain 5

Time Machine 6

Best Seat in the House 9

Collector's Corner 10

Worthy Opponents 12

Club Ways 14

On the Map 16

Kit and Crest 19

We Won! 20

For the Record 22

Soccer Words 24

Index 24

About the Author 24

Words in **bold type** are defined on page 24.

Zlatan Ibrahimovic fires up his teammates during a 2012 match. The big striker smashed all of the club's scoring records.

Meet Paris Saint-Germain

Paris is one of the oldest cities in Europe. Saint Germain is one its loveliest neighborhoods. The city's most popular soccer team is the Paris Saint-Germain Football Club. In most parts of the world, when people say "football" they are talking about the game of soccer, not American football.

Some fans call the team The Red and Blue. Others call them The Parisians. No matter what the club is called, Paris Saint-Germain always plays to win.

TIME MACHINE

In the world of soccer, Paris Saint-Germain is a very young club. It began in 1970 when two clubs in Paris joined forces to become one. By the 1980s, "PSG" was one of the best teams in all of France. By the 1990s, they were one of the best in Europe. The club's great players include **Dominique Rocheteau**, Paul Le Guen, and David Ginola.

FRANCE

DOMINIQUE ROCHETEAU

George Weah blasts a shot against Barcelona in a 1995 match.

Parc des Princes is full for a 2015 match.

BEST SEAT IN THE HOUSE

Paris Saint-Germain plays its home **matches** in Parc des Princes, which is French for Princes' Park. It is the third soccer stadium built on the same spot. The first was built in 1897. The French royal family had once used the land for hunting. That is how the field got its name. Parc des Princes holds just under 50,000 fans.

COLLECTOR'S CORNER

These collectibles show some of the best Paris Saint-Germain players ever.

SAFET SUSIC

Midfielder

1982–1991

When Susic dribbled, it seemed like he had the ball on a string. His **ball control** created scoring chances for his teammates.

BERNARD LAMA

Goalkeeper

1992–1997 & 1998–2000

Lama followed popular Joel Bats as PSG's main goalkeeper. Lama was amazing in winning the club's first European title in 1996.

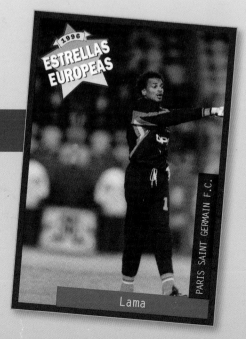

EZEQUIEL LAVEZZI

Forward

2012–2016

Lavezzi could play any position on the field. His passing and scoring helped PSG win three league titles in a row.

ZLATAN IBRAHIMOVIC

Forward

2012–2016

In four seasons, Ibrahimovic smashed every club scoring record. He had 50 goals in 51 matches during 2015–16.

THIAGO SILVA

Defender

First Year with Club: 2012

Paris fans were very happy when Silva joined the club. As team captain, he led PSG to four league titles in a row.

WORTHY OPPONENTS

The biggest soccer rivalry in France is between its two most popular teams. Paris Saint-Germain and Olympique de Marseille play in the two largest cities in France. Paris is the stylish capital in the northern part of the country. Marseille is a hard-working port city in the south. When the two teams face each other, everything in France seems to come to a stop.

PSG's Angel Di Maria dribbles past an Olympique de Marseille defender during a 2016 match.

13

CLUB WAYS

Not all fans of Paris Saint-Germain are fans of the soccer team. Like many sports clubs in Europe, PSG also has teams in other sports. The club has a champion handball team. The players wear the same uniforms as the soccer team. PSG has an eSports team, too. It competes in *League of Legends* and *FIFA* soccer video game tournaments.

The Paris Saint-Germain eSports team practices for a *FIFA 17* video game tournament.

ON THE MAP

Paris Saint-Germain brings together players from many countries. These are some of the best:

1. **Luis Fernandez** • Tarifa, Spain
2. **Safet Susic**
   Zavidovici, Bosnia and Herzegovina
3. **Mustafa Dahleb** • Bejaia, Algeria
4. **Francois M'Pele**
   Brazzaville, Republic of the Congo
5. **Carlos Bianchi** • Buenos Aires, Argentina
6. **Edinson Cavani** • Salto, Uruguay
7. **Thiago Motta** • Sao Bernardo do Campo, Brazil

FRANCE

LUIS FERNANDEZ

NORTH

WEST EAST

SOUTH

MAP OF EUROPE

Paris Saint-Germain's home stadium is in Paris, France.

WORLD MAP

Lucas Moura wears the club's home kit, which features a bright red Eiffel Tower on its crest.

KIT AND CREST

The club's uniform has always used red, white, and blue. These are the colors of the French flag. In the 1970s, the president of the team was a famous fashion designer named Daniel Hechter. He made a stylish **kit** for the players. Hechter also had the idea to put the Eiffel Tower on PSG's crest. The Eiffel Tower is the tallest structure in Paris.

WE WON!

During the 1995–96 season, Paris Saint-Germain was one of 32 clubs playing in the Cup Winners' Cup. The tournament brings together the cup winners from European leagues. PSG won one close match after another and reached the final. They beat Rapid Wien of Austria in the championship game, 1–0. Bruno N'Gotty scored the winning goal.

Bernard Lama makes a stop during a 1996 match. His saves during the Cup Winners' Cup tournament made the difference for Paris Saint-Germain.

21

FOR THE RECORD

These stars have won major awards while playing for Paris Saint-Germain:

1985   Luis Fernandez • France Football Player of the Year

1992   Alain Roche • France Football Player of the Year

1993   David Ginola • France Football Player of the Year

1994   Bernard Lama • France Football Player of the Year

1995   Vincent Guerin • France Football Player of the Year

1995   George Weah • European Footballer of the Year

1995   George Weah • World Player of the Year

2015   Blaise Matuidi • France Football Player of the Year

Paris Saint-Germain has won more than 20 major championships!

French League

1985–86
1993–94
2012–13
2013–14
2014–15
2015–16

Cup Winners' Cup

1995–96

Coupe de France*

1981–82
1982–83
1992–93
1994–95
1997–98
2003–04
2005–06
2009–10
2014–15
2015–16

French League Cup

1994–95
1997–98
2007–08
2013–14
2014–15
2015–16

Blaise
Matuidi

The Coupe de France (French Cup) is the country's biggest tournament.

Soccer Words

Ball Control
The ability to shoot, pass, and change direction quickly without losing the ball to a defender.

Kit
The official league equipment of soccer players, including a club's uniform.

Matches
Another word for games. Soccer matches are 90 minutes long. Each half is 45 minutes, with a 15-minute break in between.

Index

Bats, Joel................................10
Bianchi, Carlos........................16
Cavani, Edinson.......................16
Dahleb, Mustafa.......................16
Di Maria, Angel........................**13**
Fernandez, Luis...........16, **16**, 22
Ibrahimovic, Zlatan.........**4** , 11, **11**
Ginola, David.......................6, 22
Guerin, Vincent........................22
Hechter, Daniel........................19
Lama, Bernard...........10, **10**, 21, 22
Lavezzi, Ezequiel................11, **11**
Le Guen, Paul...........................6
Matuidi, Blaise....................22, **23**
Motta, Thiago...........................16
Moura, Lucas...........................**18**
M'Pele, Francois.......................16
N'Gotty, Bruno.........................20
Roche, Alain............................22
Rocheteau, Dominique.............6, **6**
Silva, Thiago.......................11, **11**
Susic, Safet................10, **10**, 16
Weah, George....................**7**, 22

Photos are on **BOLD** numbered pages.

About the Author

Mark Stewart has been writing about world soccer since the 1990s, including *Soccer: A History of the World's Most Popular Game.* In 2005, he co-authored Major League Soccer's 10-year anniversary book.

About Paris Saint-Germain F.C.

Learn more at these websites:
www.psg.fr/en/Accueil/0/Home
www.fifa.com
www.teamspiritextras.com